La Doña:

Essays on the Dominican Matriarch

Edited by Yamberlie M. Tavarez

DWA Press is an Imprint of Dominican Writers Assoc., a 501 (c) (3) non-profit literary arts organization founded in 2015 with the mission to support Dominican writers by providing them the tools and resources to become published authors.

Editor: Yamberlie M. Tavarez
Spanish Mechi Anais
Cover Art Design: Angela Abreu
ISBN-9781737246770

Published in the United States.

DWA Press
An imprint of Dominican Writers Assoc.
www.dominicanwriters.com
info@dominicanwriters.com

For the matriarchs.
The ones who loved, shaped, and
inspired us. Para mi doña,
Ercilia Catalina Roque de Acosta
"Abuela"
1942-2015

CONTENTS

MAMI

Abril Peña

Driving from La Capital to San Francisco de Macorís in a borrowed white Honda Civic, my youngest brother asleep in the backseat, me in the passenger seat grasping onto every gust of cool air coming out of the AC vent, and mami anxiously clutching the steering wheel while deciphering traffic signs.

We're lost.

This is the first time I've ever seen mami drive a car in her country. Whenever we visit the Dominican Republic, she's no longer the mom who hauls her kids in a Toyota Sienna minivan throughout Queens, New York, but rather a tourist in her motherland, gripping the grab handle in the passenger seat, shaking her head as we weave through traffic and motorcycles and clouds of dust. "Es demasiado peligroso manejando aquí," she clamors every time.

We've barely been on speaking terms. As soon as our plane touched down in Santo Domingo, we had an unspoken agreement to play nice and put on this illusion that we have our shit together as a family for mamá, for the distant relatives, and the family friends. They have no idea that mami and I were having screaming matches just weeks prior over trivial things like dirty dishes or significant things like her buying a house with her boyfriend. They don't know that we can't even sit in family therapy without competing in the trauma Olympics, in which there is no winner.

No, they know none of that.

They only know of us as the smiling faces on their Facebook feed—the graduations, the birthdays, the vacations, and the chismes they hear through voice memos in the WhatsApp group chats. They know mami as the architect, the stoic single mother, the career woman, the bohemian who listens to Latin American folk music, whose Facebook statuses are poetic, political, and absent of grammatical errors. The mami they know may look somewhat familiar to me, but I don't know her.

The mami I know criticizes the kink of my hair, the boyish sneakers I wear, the vulgar music I listen to, and the attention I get from my reverberating laugh. She suppresses the few things I have in common with her and the many things that remind her of papi. She kills her curls in a fresh blowout and questions why I let mine live. When people ask her how I'm doing, she doesn't tout that I'm finishing my degree while working part-time; she sneers, *"ella no hace nada."* To her, I do nothing, nothing in comparison to what she does.

A martyr of motherhood is the role that has defined her identity, whether she likes it or not. She uses her words to hurt me, and I defend myself using the same voice I inherited from her. Suddenly I'm rebellious, defiant. "You are not a good daughter," she tells me, "not like I was. I used to cook for my father and make coffee without being asked. I listened to my mother. I never disrespected her!" By this point in the lecture, my bedroom door has already been shut behind me.

She's tough, mami. But not as tough as her mother.

Whenever we are in el campo at mamá and papá's house, the beautiful home where they raised their children and returned to for retirement after working for decades in New York, mami is no longer the architect, the career woman, the bohemian—she's boiled down to the obedient daughter. She happily runs to make papá another cup of coffee while he sits in his rocking chair listening to classical music on the porch. In the sala, she opens up a maleta full of new dresses, shoes, pants, and shirts for mamá to inspect and distribute amongst the family members, according to size and needs, ultimately to be disappointed that mami didn't bring more.

She bickers with mamá about the things that have been misplaced since the last time we were here or how yet another girl quit working in the house because mamá was difficult. "Las dominicanas no quieren trabajar," mamá says in her defense before mami is tasked with hiring another

Dominican girl to cook and clean, hopefully, one who hasn't heard of mamá's bad reputation with the help.

The imperfections of me and my brother—his unkempt Afro hair and my acne—are blamed on mami. She explains how she begged and pleaded with my brother to go to the barbershop before the trip and how many soaps and treatments she's bought for me that failed to clear up my skin. Uninterested in explanations or excuses, mamá has already left the room. She drops bombs of criticism on Mami, and her sisters alike, going before the debris settles.

My Goliath suddenly shrinks down and becomes David.

It's bizarre to see mami like this, demeaning and being ordered around. The target has been removed from my back and promptly placed on mami's. Her jaw-clenching after every conversation with mamá only begins to soften when she sits alongside papá en la galeria.

Even though I'll get the occasional lecture from mamá, mostly about how I should be sending her more money since I work a "good" job or that I should be more respectful towards my mother, the lectures mami gets in private are much harsher. For mami, my failures are compounded on top of hers.

In the car, I am holding mami's phone, trying to navigate using Google Maps with a single signal bar. We stop to ask men in flip flops and worn Old Navy T-shirts for directions, but we end up even more lost than before. We reach a toll bridge, and mami asks the young morenita in the booth if this road goes to Villa Tapia, and she replies, "No señora, tienes que dar la vuelta y devolverte." She gave us directions and let us go through without paying so we could head back on the road.

The silence in the car felt unfamiliar. It wasn't the usual silence, thick with tension after an argument or an annoyance. Mami looked zoned out like she wasn't in her body anymore. Eventually, she broke the silence to point out places that she knew, where she and her college friends used to hang out, and where her favorite aunt and uncle lived.

She sounded different too. She spoke softly, almost in a whisper, as if she was having a private conversation with herself about her memories, and I just happened to overhear. In between directing turns and merges, I asked her why she decided to leave the Dominican Republic and go to New York. It was a question I had never thought to ask before this moment, but it felt like the only chance I'd have to ask her before we assumed our usual oppositional positions.

She was quiet, and for a moment I thought maybe she hadn't heard me . Finally, she said, "I felt too big for this little island."

The words stood still between us. Until this moment, I didn't realize how little I knew about mami. I don't know her in the way that papi knows her, her friends know her, her sisters, boyfriend, or colleagues know her. I don't know how she became mami, who she was before she was mami, or who she wishes she could be instead of mami. I don't know what keeps her up at night besides the menopausal sweats. I don't know who her first heartbreak was or when she felt the freest.

As a teenager, I used to snoop through mami's room to find information, something to piece together the mystery that is my mother. I would find the small pieces of paper with her New Year's Resolution goals, a letter her ex-boyfriend wrote to her, or a list of her passwords in her notebook. I couldn't ask her to tell me more about herself because it required a level of vulnerability we wouldn't allow ourselves to enter, and I didn't want her to know that I wanted to know.

I wondered if the expectations placed on her weighed as heavy as the ones she put on me. I wondered if, given the opportunity, she would go back and make any changes, changes that would mean my brother and I wouldn't exist, and even so, if she would have the courage to admit it to herself. I wondered about the times she yelled at me, if she was just envious of the willpower I had to fight back in the ways that she didn't dare to at my age.

She doesn't share much about herself that didn't add to the surface-level portrayal of what she wanted people to see: the stoic single mother, the bohemian, the architect. In this white Honda Civic in the Dominican Republic and the Toyota minivan in New York, I don't know who the woman driving was.

I didn't know anything about mami, but I knew she was too big for this little island.

ODE TO MAMÁ

Amanda M. Ortiz

My abuela was a woman of many apodos, but to her children, to her grandchildren, to me, she was and will forever be, "*mamá.*" Beloved for her unwavering fierceness, her gracious heart, and her radiant beauty, she was equally despised for these same qualities, among others. One couldn't have just lukewarm feelings towards or about her. Her very existence demanded a definitive stance—a testament to who she was, if there ever was one.

As a child I became a collector of shelved trinkets she had once gifted others (namely, my siblings and my mom), that they weren't too reluctant to part with: a nearly empty, rose-colored ballerina perfume bottle; a small silver ring with a turquoise stone; clip-on, faux gemstone earrings; a black wool beret. These seemingly unremarkable keepsakes took on great significance for me and became immediate fixtures in my personal trove of childhood treasures. In my mind, the fact that she had purposefully presented these items to others meant that the recipients held a place in her heart. And so, without any mementos from her of my own, I rationalized that me being in possession of them now meant that sentiment extended to me. This was but one of the ways she came to define some of my earliest memories, even without being physically present.

I've spent more of my life without her than with her, so she has often felt more mythical than flesh and bone. Barely of walking age when she died, I cannot recall the sound of her voice, her signature scent, or the feel of her hands. I've instead had to rely on photos and the cuentos of others to fill in the gaps. One of my mom's most cherished possessions, while I was growing up, was a sepia, framed portrait of mamá that hung prominently on a wall of our living room. I often found myself transfixed in that living room by that photo for long stretches of time, unwittingly seeking answers. Beyond being captivated by how undeniably stunning she was, I was desperate for it to somehow convey insight into *who* she was. Even in print, her presence commanded a room.

In that portrait, mamá was a whole vibe: staring assuredly at the camera, a playful smile dancing on her lips that never fully materialized. Her general forma de ser and style gave an aura of effortlessly chic (a trademark of hers, I'm told): a powder blue sleeveless top hugging her shoulders, hair coiffed in a flawless updo, drop earrings adorning her ears, matching necklace resting on her collarbone. Everything from her expression to the circumstances surrounding the portrait exuded an air of allure and mystery. I still don't know her actual age in that photograph, though if I had to guess, I'd say her early 20s. Reminiscent of how others have long described the Mona Lisa, I'm convinced there's much that immortalized señora could have learned from my abuela. Much to my disappointment at the time, the portrait never delivered the answers I longed for. Instead, it sent me on a lifelong quest to glean the real her from the lore, the nostalgia, and, at times, the vitriol with which she's been spoken of over the years.

So, what have I learned in that time—what rings most true? Demure shrinking violet, she was not. But bold and classy? Always. Vanity was not her vice, and she wasn't one to weaponize her beauty, but many describe her as the type of mujer de bandera who regularly stopped traffic. Her penetrating gaze could communicate whole paragraphs. She unabashedly stood up for and with others—loved ones and strangers alike, even when she stood alone. She faced the future resolutely, with her eyes fixed on what lay ahead, even when she had no idea where the road was taking her. And she somehow managed to do it with poise, never letting on to any ounce of fear that may have attempted to overtake her. "Una mujer con los zapatos bien puestos," as the saying goes. She was a force. She had an inability to sit quietly by and not call out wrongdoing, even in those she loved most—consequences be damned. She had a temper and let her sentiments be known but was quick to forgive. Her love for her family, those who became her family, and for her patria, was fervent and steadfast. And she was a fighter, right to the end.

It's inconceivable that she died at just 52, but in that short time, she managed to live so much life—one that took her from her frontera pueblito of Bánica to San Juan de la Maguana atop a burro with one of her siblings at the age of 5, to la capital at 15, and finally to New York in her early 30s in an effort to evade Trujillo's insidious reach. The unthinkable betrayals and loss she endured here are often beyond comprehension. She fought with all she had for the sake of her children's very survival in the face of sudden abandonment and destitution far from home, defying seemingly insurmountable odds with full decks stacked against her. In the 35 years she's been gone, those that loved her still speak her name with wistfulness and reverence. I've witnessed some of those same people sob as though suddenly afflicted anew with the reawakened depths of her absence, as if her passing were a perpetual wound instead of a mere residual scar. I've heard more than one of no blood relation refer to her as their hermana del alma.

Four of her bisnietas, none of whom she had the opportunity to meet, bear her name. I wonder every day what she would think of what our family has become, of our connections to and dissociations from each other. How different would we be as individuals, as a collective, had she lived? I imagine how her heart would have shattered to pieces witnessing the ongoing ways in which her beloved patria shamelessly brandishes its soiled hands. And not least of all, I wonder if I make her proud.

Loving abuelos have the potential to be the living embodiment of our raíces and can be such an irreplaceable resource for family history and memory. The lack of them in my own life has always been something I've mourned, and a haven I've coveted. I've long wished I could feel mamá by my side. That her survival and, by extension, her intervention somehow could have prevented or, at least, mended the brokenness that lingers.

I now know that nothing short of having her here would satisfy me, that my search for her will never reach a true conclusion. My longing to know her and love her in the flesh, to feel the reassurance of her guidance, her wisdom, her presence, will never be fully sated because those circumstances can never be.

On occasions I'm told I resemble her in mannerism or expression, this often reduces me to tears. It's difficult to fathom that I could bear any resemblance to such a dama, but it is somehow an affirmation that she is etched in me inherently. And in that way, even in the times it feels less than true, I carry her with me always.

MAMÁ TINA
DOÑA TINA

Ana María González Puente

Cuando yo nací, mis padres estaban separados y antes de yo cumplir el año, divorciados.

Mi madre, para los demás doña Patricia, se convirtió en una madre soltera de ocho niños en un país donde no existía sección ocho ni nueve ni diez y mucho menos daban cupones de alimentos.

Para suerte suya y la de su prole, en la familia existía una matriarca. Esa era mi abuela. Mamá Tina para mí y doña Tina para los vecinos y amigos.

Mamá Tina se encargaba de arreglarle la vida a todos los de su entorno con consejos prácticos, ayuda económica, un plato de comida caliente y hasta una muda. Enviudó muy joven durante la tiranía de Trujillo y para mantener a sus hijos tenía una pensión fonda en su casa de El Seibo. Allí vivían el fiscal venido de otro pueblo mientras traía a su familia si estaba casado, cualquier inspector de la Secretaría de Agricultura u otra dependencia del Gobierno. Otros transeúntes iban a desayunar y/o almorzar como los jóvenes del Cuerpo de Paz.

Para éstos siempre estaba presta con un fogón encendido, una olla hirviendo, un tajo de carne seca en el cordel del pasillo frente a la cocina, un aguacate maduro a la mano.

Cuando su hija Patricia se divorció, mamá Tina le cedió tres habitaciones y le dio tres consejos. El primer consejo fue que tuviera mucho cuidado con salir sola a bares porque la iban a desacreditar como mujer. Sí, eran esos tiempos en los sesenta donde la reputación de una mujer estaba sujeta al qué dirán. El segundo fue que buscara trabajo como oficinista, pues para algo era taquígrafa-mecanógrafa. El tercero era quizás el más difícil de ejecutar. Le dijo que le entregara los varones al papá y ella se quedara con las hembras.

–Tú no puedes quedarte con este reguero de muchachos y el buen pendejo gozando de la vida –declaró doña Tina.

Esto nunca ocurrió.

Mamá Tina crió cinco hijos y no se sabe cuántos nietos incluyendo dos nietas que una hija le dejó por unas horas porque tenía que ir a hacer una diligencia a la capital. Todavía la están esperando.

Mamá Tina se levantaba a las cinco de la mañana y prendía el fogón con las brasas que había guardado entre cenizas la noche anterior. Cuando uno de sus hijos quiso comprarle una estufa le dio un no rotundo y para suavizarlo dijo que las estufas junto con el tanque de gas explotan y ella no quería una desgracia en su casa.

Nuestra matriarca tenía las uñas de las manos negras de bregar con el carbón, agarrar las brasas de un anafe y soltarlas en el otro como si no quemaran. También de pelar plátanos, yuca llena de tierra y otros víveres.

Algunas tardes, hacía dulces de leche y de naranja, masitas y pan. Era un verdadero placer estar en su casa. Podía ser estricta y cariñosa a la vez, según las circunstancias. Conmigo en particular era muy tierna.

Después de la faena de la cocina se sentaba en la galería a leer el periódico, pues le gustaba estar informada. Entre secciones y secciones tomaba tiempo para sentarme en sus piernas, acariciaba mi pelo y me preguntaba si quería un pedazo de dulce de leche con masita. Manjar de los dioses.

Con el tiempo y gracias a su diligencia, mi madre, doña Patricia, empezó a trabajar en el Distrito Escolar del pueblo. Mamá Tina le aconsejó, o le dio órdenes porque sus consejos eran más órdenes que ejecutar, de que jugara un san. Arregló para que le dieran un número bajito para que pudiera mudarse a su propia casa. Dicho y hecho. Al poco tiempo nos mudamos, aunque no muy cerca de la abuela para las distancias de pueblo.

Mi madre era muy celosa y protectora de sus hijas. Después que nos mudamos, me costaba sacar permiso para ir a visitar a mi mamá Tina. En una ocasión que por fin lo conseguí, mamá Tina preguntó por qué hacía varios días que no la visitaba. Le conté que no me daban permiso.

–Yo hablo con ella. No te apures –dijo.

Ni corta ni perezosa me llevó de regreso a casa. Al ver a mi madre, sin saludos protocolares, le entró diciendo algo así como que la niña me ha contado que no le quieres dar permiso para visitarme.

–¿A qué se debe esta negativa? –preguntó doña Tina a doña Patricia.

La última no supo qué contestar.

La matriarca exigió que se me dejara ir a visitarla cuantas veces yo quisiera, pues su casa no era una de citas y yo no corría ningún peligro. A partir de ese día los permisos fueron concedidos al acto.

Estoy segura que a mi progenitora no le gustó que la delatara ante su propia madre.

Cuando yo tenía cinco años participé en un certamen para elegir una reina y varias princesas con el objetivo de recaudar fondos para el Club Faro de Hicayagua. Mamá Tina me enseñó cómo debía dirigirme a los adultos para conseguir que compraran boletos.

–Primero les pide permiso con una sonrisa y cuando te lo conceden, les dice del reinado y que deseas que contribuyan –repitió varias veces.

Ella era la persona más alegre contando a diestra y siniestra que su nieta iba a ser por lo menos princesa de la alegría en el reinado a celebrarse durante las fiestas patronales de mayo.

Cuando necesitas a la matriarca ella dice presente, pero cuando habla, la escuchas o la pierdes.

Cuando mi madre perdió su trabajo de empleada pública a causa del cambio de gobierno, la matriarca consideró que ya nada hacía en el pueblo y mejor era mudarse a la capital a comenzar una nueva vida y que mis hermanos pudieran ir a la universidad si así lo deseaban.

Siempre conocía a alguien, siempre sabía con quién hablar y pedir favores que sabía pagar a su debido tiempo. Para esta ocasión desencamó a un primo militar que habían trasladado a la frontera e iba a alquilar su casa en el ensanche Ozama en la capital. Arregló todo y en pleno año escolar pusieron todos los motetes en un camión y nos mudamos -sin darnos cuenta- a la capital de la República.

Yo tenía diez años cuando esta mudanza tuvo lugar y ¡vaya mudanza! Tuve un choque cultural enorme. Los capitaleños se presentaban reservados frente a la apertura y jovialidad de los seibanos.

En general todo salió bien en Santo Domingo. Una matriarca siempre sabe lo que es mejor para los suyos.

En los atardeceres no extrañaba a mis amigas y compañeras de la escuela. No. Extrañaba a mi mamá Tina. Su ternura, su afán por hacerme sentir querida, mimada, a pesar de tener a una madre soltera ocupándose de todo, de todos y de nadie en particular.

Recuerdo que cada semana y hasta dos veces por semana, recibíamos un paquete que nos mandaba con un chofer. Ese paquete era el equivalente a un ducado, a una remesa. Esperado con ansia para saciar las necesidades perentorias de las cuales ella no era ajena. Podías encontrar de todo en esos paquetes, desde un buen trozo de pan de maíz hasta una fundita amarrada con hilo de tejer con algún efectivo dentro. Cuando llegaba un paquete se nos alegraba el alma y se nos llenaba el estómago.

Ese mismo primer año cuando terminaron las clases me mandó a buscar con el chofer del pueblo para pasarme unas semanas con ella. Entonces la vi pequeña, reducida, caminando lenta. Por primera vez noté sus canas y su moño sujetado con dos ganchos. También noté su sonrisa que dejaban ver sus dientes postizos y las arrugas en la comisura de su boca fina y amplia.

Me abrazó al llegar y me hizo su pregunta favorita: ¿tienes hambre?

Cuando regresé a la capital, llevaba conmigo una funda de papel con cinco mil pesos para el inicial de una casa que mamá Tina le mandaba a mi madre. Yo era una niña todavía, pero ella me dio esa responsabilidad.

–Usted no le dice a nadie lo que lleva. Cuando llegue se lo entrega a su mamá y regresa mañana otra vez para acá.

Ya hablé con ella y con el chofer –dijo segura de sí misma como siempre.

Varias veces volví a El Seibo para verla, para escuchar su voz, para sacar la cédula. La última vez que la vi con vida la habían trasladado a la capital para tratarle unas dolencias que seguramente eran achaques de la edad. Fui a visitarla a la clínica Rodríguez Santos. Le sujeté las manos. Entreabrió los ojos y me regaló una sonrisa con toda la fuerza que pudo su cuerpo afligido y moribundo.

A los pocos días, fue llevada a El Seibo para que muriera en su casa como era su deseo. Como buena matriarca había dispuesto con suficiente antelación todo lo concerniente a su sepelio.

Quiso ser velada en su casa como era la usanza en sus tiempos. Nada de funerarias.

Yo no estuve presente en el preciso momento en que partió de este mundo, pero sí me trasladé de la capital a El Seibo para asistir a su velatorio y posterior traslado a su última morada después de la misa de cuerpo presente.

Descansa en paz, mamá Tina.

SE FUE LA LUZ

Catherine Ventura

As children, my brothers, cousins, and I spent our summers in the Dominican Republic with our grandmother, mamá Natalia. Each year, we U.S.-born grandkids were rounded up with our maletas and sent off to the island. Annual trips that perhaps were deemed vital by our struggling parents, who went above and beyond to ensure we remained tethered to the roots from which they bore us.

In those days, mamá Natalia lived in La Villa, a small apartment—half home, half marquesina—in the city of Santiago. Blue, green, beige and bright pink buildings lined up against the horizon. The boundaries of the apartment's marquesina were marked by bars de hierro that, like vines, climbed up and down all windows and doorways, separating this space from the outside world.

In the evenings, just as the sun would begin descending, the power would go out. As if this didn't happen twice a day, *every day*, shouting voices would travel from all over the village: "*Se fue la luuuuuuz*!" mamá Natalia would explain to us the sort of people, la gente con dinero, that could afford backup generators to make up for the lack of infrastructure that caused these apagones—blackouts that stretched across portions of each day in the Dominican Republic.

During those years, *se fue la luz* meant trying my best to fall asleep inside an inescapable heat and humidity that taunted me for what it seemed to know: that I was not born on its tierra, not made of the same substance, not yet resilient enough to withstand consistent discomfort. *Se fue la luz* meant hearing the chatter of my teeth and trying to quell my body's shivers with a little dance in the bathtub while a single stream of cold water—with no way of heating itself—traveled through a pipe and onto the top of my head. *Se fue la luz* meant all of us kids gathering every night on la marquesina, waiting for the breeze that would occasionally pass and cool us off as the sky grew darker—waiting for the stories.

As soon as we heard the village's voices, we'd race to the front of the apartment, hoping to get the best chair of the few available. Excitedly, we would recite a line we'd inherited from la doña's collection of sayings: *El se que se va de villa, pierde la silla.* Upon taking our places, we'd see the others making their way towards us, children that lived in La Villa whom we had befriended and who would come to gather with us to hear doña Natalia's stories. Sure enough, as soon as the sun said its final goodbye, mamá Natalia would gracefully take her seat on her rocking chair and begin whichever story she had for us that night.

She told stories of the witches she knew in her day and how they were treated by Dominican society. Of the atrocities endured by las hermanas Mirabal. Of Trujillo's dictatorship and how he elicited a fear felt in every moment, in every interaction, but that few dared to name out loud. Of la Ciguapa, a creature of Dominican folklore, whose backward feet, exposed blue skin, and long, pitch-black hair I dreamt of for many nights after.

On that marquesina, during those summer nights that remain untainted by time, she told us stories we didn't know we needed. Ones we didn't even realize we longed to hold as shards of knowledge. Fragments that, years later,—many years after mamá Natalia ceased to be with us in earthly form—we'd try to remember. To gather her knowing's. To call whatever we made of it our own.

On the island's tierra, we created worlds that still live tethered to a nostalgic place within us. An expansiveness of space as rich as it is empty, like the landscape of our grandmother's home in La Villa and the vastness of our uncle's land near el rio en Inoa. These grounds were fertile for our tender imaginaries, for the play we engaged in. Yet, the island's earth has not forgotten us. Still, through my memories, she beckons me.

Back in the States, the distance between the two worlds we straddled felt stark. Our lives had already begun molding us, acclimating our senses to the congestion and air of urgency that permeated Paterson, NJ, the city I'd been raised in. Mami worked tirelessly—en el afan, as she used to say—to single-handedly support the three of us in an unfamiliar place that had promised so much. With grief and grace, she faced new fears and fought fresh battles for too many of our childhood years.

Our first cramped apartment on Madison Ave offered us, at least, a place to share. Another place to call home. *Gracias a Dios!* we were made to remember. *Amen*, mami would often say to herself, each time she'd call on God's grace to provide the strength she needed. *Si Dios quiere*, we were made to remember whenever we made plans or wishes, no matter how trivial.

When we'd forget to acknowledge God's role in the unfolding of our lives, there was the voice of mamá Natalia or that of our mother: *Si Dios quiere*. Two decades later, the voice—now channeled through another woman—still speaks the truths we were made to remember. That voice, now, is my own.

In La Villa, I'd spend so many moments wondering why I didn't see buildings with vibrant colors in the States. Wishing that my nose could somehow store the island's distinct smell: humidity, gasoline, leña, endurance, and joy, all at once, I would keep my maleta stuffed with the same clothes that had touched that world I was already homesick for. *Si Dios quiere*. I'd hope that, in their fibers, I might somehow find my way back to that feeling—that place of possibility where I dreamed of new worlds to call home.

DECODING LA DOÑA'S LOVE

Elinol López

Porque mami ha vivido una vida dura, una vida que nunca ha sido de ella. Y aun así se le agradece.

I met mami when I arrived in the US in April of 1999. She met me when she birthed me four years earlier.

Just 15 days after I was born, she found herself living in New York, huddled in a crowded one-bedroom apartment and working odd jobs. Papi's papers hadn't come through.

As an immigrant, sparse on funds and obstructed by language and education, her best option to ensure our survival was to send my two-year-old sister and me off to her campo in the Dominican Republic. She worked to build a solid foundation for us in the US., navigating a harsh new world while we were being cared for by family. Mami welcomed us once papi was allowed to travel and she had landed an apartment in Washington Heights.

The memory of walking into that sala lingers heavily in my mind. Tall beige walls and glossy hardwood tiles disappeared behind the cheering crowd of strangers. The blaring music muffled their words as, one by one, they introduced themselves as my tios, tias, y primos. Confused and overwhelmed by the newness of this place, my sister and I clung to each other. Dizzying notes of powder perfume, beer, and Old Spice engulfed me with every hug. Although a scary moment for four-year-old me, the lasting impression has grown warm over time, and I would eventually come to know these men, women, and children as my family.

The most joyful stranger in the room was crying, smiling, flowing with overwhelming love. She introduced herself as my mami. That very moment remains one of the happiest I've seen her in all the years since.

Once reunited, she struggled to connect with me. As a child who had just been uprooted from one home to another, from one lengua to another, from one mami to my other, my behavior during those early days consisted of shying away from her and crying about missing my other mother. I was homesick and angry. And because I wouldn't connect with her emotionally, she had to pour her motherly love into tending to my physical well-being: feeding me, clothing me, brushing my hair. By the time I warmed up to her, we had developed a cryptic language that relied heavily on acts of service as subtle displays of love rather than overt physical affection and words of affirmation. I would sometimes sit next to her on the couch and place her arm around me in my search for closeness.

I have a bad habit of remembering her as unsmiling and laconic. Pero mami cuido muy bien a sus niñas. She took us to the park in the afternoons, stayed on the bench for hours while we ran around, and sat with her silence. When she couldn't find a sitter, she'd take us downtown to her job, doing laundry in a restaurant basement. We'd stop at Rite Aid and browse magazines and toys on the way, then buy orange Trident and pink Snapple. I loved watching cartoons while folding napkins and tablecloths, knowing she was near.

When I was in high school, she'd spend nights going with me from Starbucks to McDonald's to the hospital emergency room so that I could use the Wi-Fi to finish my assignments. Then she'd brew me coffee and make me platanos con salami before I left for school, shouting from the window, "no te duermas en el tren," as I walked away.

I rarely called her when I went off to college. This time it was I who separated myself for four years. Academia, where I thrived, was a foreign arena to her. I didn't know how to communicate my accomplishments to her in a way that made sense. I knew she was proud, but it felt lacking and incomplete. She couldn't articulate exactly what she was proud of. So I retreated into my pain and stopped looking for ways to connect with her.

I wonder if she feels the same way about her daughters. How we can't fully appreciate her or express exactly what we are proud of because we don't truly understand the depth of her accomplishments. When we try to acknowledge all that she's been through and how grateful we are, we can only touch the surface of her experience. Her struggle is foreign to us. She's alone there, loving us and leading us. And we, the benefactors of her sacrifices, feel guilt. We mistakenly thought we were walking a path that leaves her behind when she's the one who's paved it.

As I grew older, I learned that every chapter of mami's life had involved sacrifice. She was born to parents who could not nourish her and entrusted her life to the care of their neighbors. She, too, was mothered by another. As an adolescent, she was pulled from school and made to labor for her family's finances. She was later strategically married off to travel to America, while my father stayed behind.

Every choice she made was for reasons beyond her. She wasn't allotted the privilege of nonconsequential pursuit; of picking up a hobby out of sheer curiosity, then dropping it for a new one, reading a book or watching a new movie on opening night, or trying a recipe she found on the internet. Her most trivial pastimes seem to be window-shopping when the days get warm and napping on the couch en la tardecita after a long day of diligencias. This sacrificial pattern has been repeated since before I was born, when she separated from her children to work, when she dragged her children to work with her. That is what she knew to do to provide.

I used to think of her life as a thief. As though she's some drained, hollowed woman. I still struggle with the knowledge that she has endured hardships I will never understand. But that's the thing, mami gives. She gives with purpose, proudly, and gladly. It fulfills her.

Porque mami ha vivido una vida que ha sido de ella, sin remordimiento.

COLUMNA SOFOCADA

Gina Arias

My childhood summers were spent in the Dominican Republic at the home of my maternal grandparents, with an almost complete lack of adult supervision. The days opened with the distant crow of roosters and were filled with a rhythm of my own making.

Breakfast was usually warm, oval *pan de agua* spread with creamy melted butter and thin slices of delicious farm cheese, always laid out in ceramic plates covered by other ceramic plates. A small metal mug of sweet café con leche to wash it all down.

The bread was purchased only moments before from a young bread seller who roved the neighborhood on foot announcing himself "*Panadero*! *Panadero*!" carrying his fresh-out-the-oven product in an enormous basket covered with a light cotton cloth. Reaching into her ample bosom my grandmother, mamá, would pull out a worn, black leather change purse with a golden clasp, from which to pay the boy, but not before she criticized something about the quality of the day's bread or its price or the late hour at which he was peddling it. It was hard to please mamá.

Maria del Pilar Arias Guerrero, mamá to us, and doña Pilar to everyone else, was a serious, reserved woman. She could, at brief turns, be affectionate and perceptive but was, in general, a woman who frowned often.

My grandmother was very fair-skinned. Full of pride she let it be known that her family had descended from Spain, with blue eyes no less! Despite the delusion of white supremacy with which she was raised, and which she fed her entire life as if it was a precious poodle, she fell deeply in love with a man of African descent. My grandfather, eleven years her senior, was not conventionally handsome but was blessed with captivating charm and swagger. What is known as Black in the United States, in DR, his particular shade is called "Indio" even though there isn't a Taino to be found anywhere on the entire island.

Growing up, what my mother most heard about Black people was focused on Haitians. As a young girl, if she misbehaved, mamá would warn her that the Haitians would come to eat her, because that's what they did: eat bad children. In addition to fanning the flames of anti-Haitian sentiment that has plagued the DR, my grandmother was wildly ignorant about Blackness in general. She once told me that Blacks in Cuba were of African descent. When I asked her where she thought Black people came from in the Dominican Republic she didn't have an answer.

Mama didn't work outside of the home and truth be told, she did not work much within the home either. She bragged that in earlier times she sometimes had two women servants. Mamá bore papá twelve children, eight girls, and four boys, and they remained married for 52 years until death did them part with his passing.

Papá, on the other hand, was often away working in the twin industries of agriculture and bedding women all over the land. My grandfather had 25 children that we know of. Three of them were born before he met my grandmother, the rest, however, were born to various women during my grandparents' lengthy marriage. Papá moved in the world on his own terms, as did most men of his era, particularly those of the middle and upper classes. Both funny and endearing, within moments he was the center of any room he entered.

Mamá, however, lived with a bitterness that seethed just below the surface. Her demeanor, most often cold and dignified, belied the pedestal of adoration on which she placed my grandfather and her sons. They filled her with pride even when they disappointed her. They could do no wrong, and even when they did, her anger toward them was short-lived and surface level.

Her daughters, however, by and large, could do no right. And so I was neither doted on nor coddled by the woman in whose care I was placed for two full months of every year, making for extraordinary summers that, in later years, helped me to better understand why so many Latin American authors write in that genre known as magical realism.

Despite Pilar's lack of knowledge, in many realms, my grandmother was, in fact, quite astute. The day after the Mirabal sisters were killed, in November 1960, my grandfather read about it in the newspaper. "Look Pilar!" he called out to my grandmother. "Look at what a terrible thing has happened! Three sisters were killed in a car accident." Mamá scanned the article over his shoulder and leaned in closer to him. In a hushed tone, she responded, "That was no accident. Don't you see who they are, the Mirabal sisters! Those women were murdered by Trujillo's henchmen!" Papá said nothing, and realizing she was right only shook his head slowly in acknowledgment.

Out of self-preservation, my grandparents adhered to the rules laid out by the Trujillo dictatorship, including keeping a photo of Trujillo prominently displayed in their home with the caption "Aqui manda el jefe." However, they were staunchly against the regime. They would listen to underground radio programs on low volume in their second-floor bedroom broadcast from Cuba, by exiles who resisted Trujillo's reign.

Later in life, my grandmother, in her exasperation over the criminality, violence, and corruption exhibited by both civilians and government authorities in the Dominican Republic would exclaim "This country needs another Trujillo! In those days you could sleep with your door unlocked! Who would dare to come in and rob you? No one!" Mamá's own personal experiences with delincuencia no doubt shaped her nostalgia for the Trujillo era. Once when she was in her front yard, she had two gold chains snatched from her neck. It never helped to remind her that she had been anti-Trujillo during his rule, because eventually that became irrelevant. She came to place more value on the security afforded by an oppressive regime than the insecurity and lawlessness experienced in a democratic one.

In her early 70s, I sat down with her to get some oral history. She sat stoically rocking herself in the mecedora, her short hair fully gray, dressed in black, for the luto she carried for papá. She recounted her many home births attended by local midwives. She told of how my grandfather, noting her anger over his many escapades resulting in children with various women, said to her that he would never accept divorce as an option.

Mamá talked about her education. In the rural village where she was raised, she received lessons at an informal home-based school, up to about the 3rd grade. That was as far as the school went. Her father decided she would be sent to live with an aunt and uncle in Santiago to continue her education at a formal institution. Abruptly, for reasons unknown to her and explanations ungiven, he made an about-face on that decision. She told me that she would have liked to study medicine had she been allowed to stay in school.

Mamá married papá when she was just 17 years old, shackled for over half a century to stifling gender norms and expectations of what a married woman could be, say, and do in conservative mid-20th century Dominican society. She enjoyed class and color privileges, but also endured a lifetime subsumed under male domination and oppression. She told me her stories, in a matter-of-fact way, without any note of victimhood, sadness, or even anger. By this point in life, the necessary armor fit her snugly.

It then dawned on me why my loving and charming grandfather always smiled and laughed heartily, and as a result, was dearly loved, yet mamá, both respected and feared, perpetually furrowed her brow.

LAS DOÑAS OF MY DOMAIN

Jhoselin Perez

Quiero dedicar esta expresión a todas las mujeres de mi vida. The main ones in my life symbolize very important characteristics: Dedication to Family (abuela); Guidance (mami); Ternura (abuela Guilla) and Protection (doña Rosita).

Abuela: la patrona de mi familia.

Ahora mismo tiene104 años y está en una cama sin poder moverse mucho. But I always remember her as a strong survivor dedicated to the family.

Born in 1918, she married very young and had a son. A few years later, she remarried my grandfather, don Pupo. Abuela Fela had to move from town to town as my grandfather was a farmer and musician; you name it, he did it. And in each city, my mother, uncles, and aunts were born. They settled in the capital, Santo Domingo, where she had to endure grandpa's many infidelities that resulted in other fruits. And yet, she always kept her head high. She never complained. She never wavered; never showed her emotions.

I didn't know abuela until I arrived in New York. I don't have many memories of her when I lived in DR. I suppose I was too young to remember. My mother tells me that she was always selling something to support the family since grandpa was always away. As a woman in those days, you had to do what was needed to survive and keep your family safe. Abuela and mami are so much alike--their hair, eyes, and hands.

I do remember abuela being strong, but quiet. She wasn't tall but her presence was powerful. Respected to the core. She never lifted a finger, but boy was she tough. One word from her, and you sat down.

I remember abuela being there, helping, with love. Always taking care of me and my cousins during our Saturday get-togethers at her house; seated in the living room after making dinner and just chatting with us.

I remember her in the kitchen when we arrived from school. She always catered to all of us. Setting plates of spaghetti, mangú or tostones, or whatever each of us wanted that day. I was the one with the tostones.

Gracias Abuela.

Mami: my strength, my warrior, and the one I call my best friend.

As I walk through the doors, I encounter the familiar sounds of the spoon against the pot, the savory smells of adobo, carne, and orégano. The sound of her voice full of joy. The touch of her warm embrace, memorable. As an adult, I cherish all these details.

She is the one that taught me to smile, to be strong, to get up and not stop for anything or anyone. Mami is that constant part of my life. We share a bond that I can't imagine being without. She is mi doña.

She taught me how powerful education is even though she never finished High School. She guided me to be successful and never depend on anyone. Taught me that I can be anything I wanted, when I wanted. That the man in my life was to adore me, respect me, and love me. But that I should still be able to take care of myself.

By the time she received her visa, she had already divorced papi. She worked hard to bring me to the US on her own, bringing me to New York when I was only 10 years old.

I always saw mami learning, working, and moving. She never sits still. In DR, I recall her learning pottery to sell her creations. In NY, she went to school to learn English, got her driver's license, became a US citizen, and went to school to become a home attendant.

She worked in a hotel as a housekeeper for many years, where her English got so much better. Even now, retired, she doesn't sit still. As part of her Church community, she assists with all kinds of events. I am always telling her to stop and breathe. "I can't do that," she insists.

I am so proud of her and because of her education and guidance, I am who I am today.

Thank you, mami.

Abuela Guilla: sweet in every sense of the word.

Abuela Guilla was tiny, had dark skin, soft hands, and wrinkles. She walked slowly and wore a thin printed robe aligned with laces. She wore chancletas, those with multiple holes in the front, like a plastic net.

Abuela Guilla radiated love through her baking and just being. She was always kind; gave amazing hugs and I recall her always being there and taking time from her baking to sit with me and chat. I don't recall what we talked about. I was about 7 or 8 years old from the last memories I have of her.

When I walked up to her second-floor apartment, I could smell the sweetness, the smell of baking cakes, pastelones, or mi favorito, arepas de doña Guilla. There was always un pedazo waiting for me. She would always be standing in front of her kitchen counter, way too high for her stature, see me and say "ven mi hija, para que nos sentemos en el barcón." She would bring my piece of arepa with some refresco rojo and we would sit on her barcón on mecedoras eating with such delight. If I rocked the chair fast, she would never stop me; get crumbs all over my outfit and she would let it be.

She was my paternal grandmother (or who I thought was papi's mom). Later, I found out she was the woman that raised him as my dad's mom passed away when he was very young. Yet, I looked a lot like her. In the barrio, they would call me Guillita. She never had children of her own, but everyone in the family calls her abuela Guilla.

Gracias abuela Guilla, que en paz descanses.

Doña Rosita: mother of the love of my life.

The first time I saw doña Rosita was in the kitchen of her Bronx apartment, and to this day, that is where you would find her. Doña Rosita is what I've learned to call *la jefa de la familia*. She's the most compassionate, caring, dedicated woman, in her family.

I met Carlos in 1996 and doña Rosita welcomed me with open arms. From day one, I have always felt part of her family. She is the one cooking pots and pots of food for all occasions. Thanksgiving, Navidad, Año Nuevo, el baby shower de Ruth, el cumpleaños de Jan, toda ocasión, nunca falta la comida de doña Rosita.

She worked very hard when she was young to bring her children (all five) plus some extended family to the US. To this day, she is always helping her brothers and sisters. Always worrying about her children even though they are adults. She is una abuela apoyadora; my son's number one fan. He's forever her bebito.

She took care of him when he was born while I worked a full-time job. She takes care of Jancarlos, even now that he is older. She did this with every grandchild that came her way. I never worried about dinner; she cooks for me all the time. I could always get away with my husband without worrying. Today, my husband visits her every day and we make sure she is taken care of.

All in all, she is la doña of the family. She is the protector. It doesn't matter the situation; you can't ever say anything negative about them. Not even to each other, because she will always defend the other. Her protection goes beyond her immediate family. Even my family is now under her wing.

I'm grateful to have her call me su hija.

Gracias Rosita.

La doña of my Domain: I, myself–la doña of my domain.

When I think of the concept of la doña, la patrona, la jefa, I always think of the older ones in my life. My abuela was quiet but consistently strong to keep the family united. My mother keeps my brothers in line and makes sure she is always available for her three children. Abuela Guilla, with her slow and tiny stance, provided these huge hugs and calmness in my life. Doña Rosita embraced me into her family without regret. And I believe myself la doña of my small family. My husband and my son are my world. I cater my life around them while also ensuring my own goals.

These women have taught me that family is number one, that no sacrifice is ever enough, that love goes a long way, and that we can accomplish anything. And most of all, that we are la doña of our own domain.

Gracias mis doñas.

LA REINA

Koylan Massiell Gomez

Mami, I am proud to possess your ingenuity, kindness, selflessness, resilience, and to call you my mother. You may not have come from royalty, but you are our family's warrior, goddess, and spine. You are indeed and utterly nuestra reina.

For as long as I could remember,
my mom wore a crown. Hell,
her name is Reina.

Born on el Día de los Reyes,
already predestined for
royalty. Pero en el campo, there are no royals.

No such thing as a royal bloodline,
my mom figured, *a lo fuck it,*
she would create her own.

My mother was the first in her family to ever board an airplane when she emigrated to the United States at 23. Can you imagine this? *Una muchacha de Los Minas, de un callejon, dique viajando.*

Mami showed my siblings and me how to be resilient, persistent, and selfless. She was given the opportunity to provide a better life for her children and chose to extend that kindness to her entire family. She readily left behind her dreams in order to bring her five siblings, one by one, to the states. She wanted them to know the slums were no longer the only option.

Attaining this dream meant parting with her two toddlers, my older sister and me. Leaving us in the care of our mom's forever "ride or die," aunt Chichi, who was only 14. Chichi dropped out of High School to take care of us, and mami would spend the rest of her life trying to repay her for committing to such a noble sacrifice. It must be exhausting to know that no words or actions could ever be sufficient.

She told me her breasts were still full of milk when she came to the States—that's how young we were. She had to hand pump to relieve the physical pain of her engorged breasts. The emotional pain? Now that's something she coped with by overworking herself and taking on two jobs. When we moved to the States, she let the world know of our arrival, and she bombarded us with toys to make up for the missed birthdays, Christmas, and New Year's.

She spoke about the nights she spent alone while we were still in the Dominican Republic, separated by thousands of miles, but said it felt like two different worlds separated us. In one world, she was bombarded by Madonna's "Like a Virgin." Her daughters learned how to roll their stomachs and arch their backs to El General in another world. Neither of us knew that this cultural separation would ripple into our adult lives forever.

~❖~

Your kids need to eat,
a poem isn't gonna pay the bills. They need clothes.
An emotional breakdown isn't gonna keep them warm

from the blizzard of 96.
They need their mother,
your tears weren't going to comfort them.

My mom wasn't word-savvy, nor did she take the time to comb through her emotions. That shit is a luxury, to sit down and write what you feel, to articulate a thought when on the back of your mind was the constant drilling reminder that you were dirt poor and you weren't going to get anywhere in life if all you did was sit on your ass and dream.

For a long time, I knew mami never really had her shit together and that most of her adult life she was just pretending. She hardly buckled in front of us, and being a mother myself, I have no idea how she did it without completely losing her mind. The only emotions she expressed were extreme joy or complete seclusion. For many years she struggled with her mental health. During these early stages, when she was at the very brink of a mental health crisis, God had his way of intervening.

Chichi would always pray for her day and night. Mami says that her prayers protected her like a veil because right before she felt like she would snap, her papers came, and she left for Nueba Yol. I suppose God was trying to buy her some time. The mental health crisis still came, and not only did it come, but it rippled onto all of her children. Some of us more than others. The more I deal with my traumas, the more I feel like I am healing the wounded child in me and the traumas of many wounded children.

I loved watching my mom make yaniqueque,
the way she confidently dominated the dough
how she skillfully knew how much to knead it,

how round to roll it, how long to fry it.
Her motto was, "La comida siempre se hace con amor,
porque si no el alma lo sabe. "

Mami had the gift of bringing people together through her food. The summers were a guaranteed family reunion of sancocho and a never-ending game of Dominoes. My friends could never understand how we ate stew on scorching summer days, but the body has its way of adapting. The mangu's reminded me of our campos mudslides, and can no one tell me that the chicken from el vivero tasted the same as the pre-packaged—the audacity.

She always told me, "Mi hija, no dependa de nadie." The best thing you can do for yourself is to become fully independent. That way, no one can control you or hang anything over your head. Financial independence meant so much to her, but I knew that this economic obsession came from a place of trauma.

As a little girl, her family was so poor that she would have to clean someone's house in exchange for dinner. I wonder what that must've been like knowing that she was willingly and unwillingly throwing herself into the lion's den. Not all dinners came easy, as some houses meant she had to dodge a few pedophiles here and there. They would purposely ask for her to do the cleanings, get so close that they could take a whiff of her hair, touch her hand, graze a thigh. She either had to tolerate it or go to sleep hungry; hunger was not an option. That type of shit scars you for life.

The thing is, what choice did she have? When fight or flight is embedded in your DNA, you better work. Roll over and die? *Tu ta loca.*

Funny the things you pick up
without even knowing,
the traumas you try to break

without even trying.
It's almost like your body
is a mythical creature

because it knows
what to carry
and what to let go.

Despite all of this, I knew I came from royalty. I was raised by a strong, independent, and highly intimidating woman. Mami said that life's most challenging moments gave her the best lessons, like how to be of service to others. She always told us that the more you give, the more the universe rewards you. I felt like the universe was consistently bowing its head and kissing her feet. Like it was at her mercy. She was blessed.

I know that to this day, mami mourns the things she couldn't do, the person she couldn't become, the significant burdens she had to carry. She could not achieve a medical degree or become a backup dancer for "La Chicas del Can." For this, I am forever indebted to her because being able to live my life so freely is a direct result of what she had to give up.

I want her to know that the virtues, attributes, and affections she has instilled in her children are an incredible legacy to be proud of and will be passed down for generations.

I understand generational trauma
and extreme poverty
molded her tough exterior,

I see her softness when
preparing a meal for her family.
When she opens her door

to an immigrant relative.
When filling barrels with food
for orphaned children.

I see these acts as a way of self-healing,
I pray that one day her wounds
become so faded that the only thing left behind
is scar tissue.

EL TOQUE FINAL

Mary Gomez

The flashing silhouette of my frail, five-foot-tall grandmother, dragging her chancletas to the rhythm of her flapping purple housedress, brandishing her cooking spoon as she ran down the steep hill, was a bad omen.

This female Don Quijote conjured fears that materialized the moment she stormed through the front door and dropped to her knees in front of the vinyl orange sofa, where my mother laid catatonic, eyes wide as saucers. It was the only time I had ever seen my grandmother run that fast to rescue my mother, who otherwise exemplified courage and strength.

Not much taller than her own mother, she defied nature like the old oak tree in our backyard that battled decades of drought, flood, lightning, and hurricanes. Mami sustained the branches of our family, never bending or breaking, always holding strong.

Drought: Defying Traditions - 1963

The tiny town of El Valle is preparing for a wedding. Flower wreaths flank the main entrance to the bride's house, and the house wears pink. Tin lids hang from the almond tree past the gate and shine against the sun. The pig roasts in the backyard, and the surrounding mountains are impossibly green. The three sisters scurry about like kike mice. The oldest one is to get married, the youngest is to disappear, and Mina is always in the middle.

In the bedroom, Mina's mother orders her to assist the bride. She picks up the plain white linen dress that rests on the iron headboard and walks towards her sister, who calmly applies pink lipstick. "Too pale." Mina frowns, placing the dress on the back of the chair where her sister sits, giving her a tube of bright red lipstick.

"This would make a permanent stain on that." Her sister purses her lips and points to the dress behind her. Mina laughs loudly; "I must fulfill my duty as a handmaiden!" She bows. "And to think, we've been dating brothers this whole time, and now you and Fran are getting married." Mina smiles, bringing the dress closer to her heart.

"Yes, and if mom finds out you've been dating Vic, she'll kill you. Now stop blabbering and help me put this rag on." She impatiently extends her arms toward Mina.

All the furniture has been removed from the small living room. The four mecedoras and the ebony coffee table soak in the sun. The dining table stands against the living room wall, covered by a white crocheted cloth and topped with two vases filled with giant sunflowers. Four rustic blue wooden chairs guard the table in pairs, and their new caning resembles freshly brushed teeth.

The wedding officiant (also father of the bride) summons the attendees to take their places. The 90-degree weather forces many to seek shelter under the almond tree, as inside, there is only room for the bride, padrinos, parents, and the absent groom. People fan themselves with Panama hats, handkerchiefs, and even pieces of cardboard. Across the street, barefoot children and el loco del pueblo crane their necks to get a glimpse.

Mina peers through a gap in the wall in the bedroom and sees the groom arrive late. He half-drunkenly yells for the bride. Her sister sighs beside her for the hundredth time and glances at Mina. "*Sinverguenza.* Let's get this over with."

The father-officiant asks everyone to stand. The bedroom door opens, and the bride takes ten steps. Mina follows her, wearing her pink polka dot Sunday dress and high heels. Mina also wears her own veil—a white mantilla draped over her head. People murmur in confusion as she enters, and she shouts over them. "What? I've decided I'm getting married too." She looks to the groom's brother, standing in as the padrino, now a groom.

Vic drops his jaw to his guayabera's pockets. Mina's mother faints; her father shushes, and the bride shrugs. She takes Mina's hand, and the two walk side-by-side toward the grooms. One groom awakens from his drunken stupor; the other falls into one. The father throws his hands in the air in surrender and calls both couples to the front. The mother is revived mid-ceremony, and the celebration commences amidst chismes, whispers, dancing, and feasting.

Thirty years later, Mina and Vic explode in hysterical laughter when their granddaughter asks them to describe their wedding day.

Flood: Married Single - 1973

Three girls of her own. Same town. Same surrounding green mountains, now brown. Grandma's house wears another color. Mina sits under the almond tree that stands under the stars. This time, she wears her Sunday dress, sky blue with white trim around the neck and sleeves. Her black, curly hair is cut short and spiked; a floppy afro that fights thinning hair and protests Mina's lack of money for hairspray. She wears her only pair of heels, white hand-me-downs her best friend no longer wears. Her pale skin, white teeth, and the trims of her dress diverge from her dark curly hair, and when she throws her head back and laughs, everyone around her surrenders. Her aura grows and grows.

How does she do that? How does her beauty shine brighter than the stars twinkling through the branches of the almond tree?

I'm terribly embarrassed standing next to her. And I think that if it weren't for us, my mom would be greater than greatness. And I think that I'm holding her back from destiny because no one who looks like that, smiles like that, and captivates like that should be destined to struggle. No one like her should be tormented by her kids' hunger. No one like her should wait for letters from a husband living 1500 miles away and only have a few dollars to stretch until the following letter. No one like her should have wealthy in-laws turning a blind eye. No one like her should be fending off vultures who prey on her vulnerability. No one like her should have to go through a nervous breakdown only to have her mother rescue her from fighting the windmills. But Mina does. And being a mother is what she is destined to do. And being a mother is what she does best.

Lightning: Mother Knows Best - 1983

After lessons are learned, it is time to repay the sacrifices made. The oldest of four, I am the trophy for her wins. I am decent and respectable, and I am an educated woman. I carry the torch at home while New York is her new battle. Now she is the one 1500 miles away from us, and Brooklyn means nothing but survival.

My siblings and I are now 100 miles apart: sacrifice means education no matter the cost, and the cost is moving to Santo Domingo and living with tia Morena. My father returns a month into my first semester of college, 1500 miles across the ocean, and decides it is time for my siblings to join me in the capital. We share one room and one bed, but our love for each other can overcome anything. Father leaves again, and Mom calls every day.

I officially started la universidad as my siblings attended a private school for the first time. We soon discover the epitome of a dysfunctional family: a feeble-minded wife, an abusive and authoritarian husband, and six children as discrepant in ages as in emotional imbalance. On the first day, we're together in tia's home, her children play a strange game: after turning off the lights, they punch each other indiscriminately in the dark. Different things happen in the dark, too: their father's rage leaves them bleeding, and we learn of his changing moods from the changing colors of his wife's face.

We manage to stay away from the tsunami while my mother's calls become more frequent and inquisitive. The husband and wife stand next to me when the phone rings and the menacing looks threaten. I don't say a word, but somehow, across the Atlantic, my mother knows.

"What were you thinking?"

"I thought they should be together," my father laments.

At dusk one day, I get off the bus at the avenida after a long day at la UASD and sluggishly walk the three blocks to my aunt's house. My little sister runs to hug me, like every day when I return. My little brother, always glued to my middle sister's hip, joins in the hug yelling "mami, mami, mami," while flailing his scrawny arms and wiggling his little body, which does not remotely match his age. I am about to ask for his surrogate mother when my mom yells from the front door: "Let's go!" And just like that, Mina magically transmigrates 1500 miles to rescue us again.

Hurricane: Bravery is Strength - 2003

The cold, murky water of the ocean defies the August Palm Beach heat. Under a large, floppy hat, I dip my feet in the wading pool and listen to the last remaining voices of children before they head back to school. Among squeals, splashes, and mother's warnings, I take one last salty breath before heading back.

The disarray in the hotel room reminds me of the past week, and armed with a glass of wine, I resign myself to start packing. The phone rings, and I pick up, rehearsing my "we can't stay another day; you start school Tuesday" response in anticipation of my daughter's thousandth request to extend our vacation. My sister is on the other side. "You need to come back."

Time does not stand still; it just vanishes. My mom sits in a wheelchair only after the repeated insistence of the orderly. She searches for my eyes; I desperately avoid hers. In her most believable voice, she tries to imbue me with strength *"Con Dios todo es posible."* She stands in the way of the blow and turns her cheek toward the clenched fist of destiny. Yet a language barrier makes me the pilot of this tortuous trip, and every time a doctor describes the indescribable, she looks to me for answers. I am the one protecting her, and English is my shield. I am the one who must be brave. I am the one smiling and translating a death sentence into a hopeful tomorrow.

Three years pretending. Three years praying. Three years hoping. Three years crying. Three years laughing together, begging God for more time. Three years saying goodbye. Her heroism intensifies a hundredfold. It's irrational to think that I can fool her. She knows. And she does what she has always done. She braves the storm and feigns strength when there is none. Her branches extend, and she hugs longer and harder.

It is her granddaughter's 16th birthday.

"How many times do I have to tell you, Mina does not wear flat shoes."

"But mom-"

"I will not disfigure this beautiful gown with those hideous shoes. Bring me my heels."

She struggles to get up from the bed but refuses my sister's hand. The last round of chemotherapy was just three days ago, and her face is swollen. She looks at the image staring at her in the mirror, and asks me to touch up her makeup. "I need more red on these lips—too pale." I hand her the tube of red lipstick, and she reapplies it with one hand while removing the headscarf with the other. She slowly places the pixie-cut wig on her head and adjusts it. *"El toque final."*

I stare transfigured. She shines. She throws her head back and laughs that laugh again, and the blackness of the wig transports me right back to childhood. And at the same time, I return to the day my grandmother ran downhill to rescue her *Dulcinea,* and see myself as the new Don Quijote.

Mina's spirit has won her yet another battle. The old oak tree returns to the earth, but its acorns have germinated new ones with branches that reach the heavens. And the future is possible because of her.

MAMA SULA LAUGHS

Nivi Canela

She braided red ribbons into my hair.

Normally when I visited mama Sula, my older cousins, Mariel y Jenny, watched me on Sunday mornings.

But today was special. Today, mama Sula would take me to her iglesia. I wasn't allowed to wear anything red when I went to church with my mom back in Jersey. Going with mama Sula somehow felt more holy. Out of all her grandkids, *I* got to see how this montaña of a woman worshiped.

She balanced me firmly between herself and the moto concho driver as we zipped through La Vega, my vision a blur of dust, palm trees, blue skies, and red ribbons.

She lit a candle at the entrance of this little chapel filled with the smell of palo santo. Inside, everything glowed scarlet and gold.

Mama Sula was a teacher in the campo. Birthed six babies, including a pair of twins: my father, who lived, and his brother, who didn't. She said somebody gave him the evil eye because they envied her twins.

Always stern, this mountain. Only seemed to smile Sundays after church when her children drove in from across El Cibao to see her.

But here in her church, she sang and clapped. She smiled down on me, and it felt like a blessing.

The bigger blessing was her laugh - the one time I heard it, more than ten years later.

We were sitting by her dining room table while tia Nora and my dad prepared the café. Tia Nora insisted I was old enough to enjoy coffee with the adults now: nineteen, a mujercita. My dad said no, held me tightly in the palm of his hand, ever a frangipani. The siblings compromised - the "real" adults would drink their coffee from big white cappuccino mugs, and I from a small lime-green espresso cup.

Dialysis was draining mama Sula's energy, and she sometimes had to be hooked up to a machine. It seemed to lower her guard. Maybe that's why she said what she said.

She looked me up and down - much like she had when I turned eleven and began to grow tetitas. She took me in, a quick-witted brown pear-shape so much like tia Nora, so much like herself, and said,

"Cuando yo tenía tu edad, las señoritas no tenían las opciones que tienen ustedes."

When I was your age, young women didn't have the options you have now.

My brain started to list things I had that she couldn't: free public education, access to a four-year college on scholarship, even grad school if I wanted to go, the job market -

"No teníamos la contracepción."

We didn't have contraception.

She grins - the mischievous twin of her church smile.

"Si yo la hubiera tenido -"

If I'd had it -

A giggle from deep in her barriga bubbles up and explodes into a guffaw.

My father stomps into the kitchen doorway,

"No! She can't have novios until after she graduates college."

I hear tia Nora cackle as if she knows all my secrets. She pokes her head between my father's arm and the doorway.

"Mija, have all the novios you want. Travel the world, live your life - then, if you want, get married."

My father's tongue is as tied as the day he caught tia Nora leafing through a sex toy catalog with tio Fabio's girlfriend.

Mama Sula sweetened her coffee amply despite her diagnosis.

La profesora, a devout Catholic until the day they laid her down, insisted on enjoying life. She insisted that I do, too - wanted me to live freely, wear red ribbons in my hair, and enjoy all the sugar I wanted.

AND YET I STILL KNOW NOTHING

Susana Kuehne

When I walked into abuela's house on weekends, I remember her greeting me with a big hug and smile—so excited I had come to see her even if she had already seen me the week before.

Babies playing in the background and a loud telenovela on the small screen created the aura that nothing could go wrong while you were at abuela's. With six puppies in her backyard, a chicken, and some storage she was holding for a random cousin, it felt like I was in another world.

Abuela could walk around in a bata and hair rollers and still exude confidence. Everyone made time to listen; her actions commanded the attention of everyone in the room. Her seven kids worshipped her (commitments to their work, spouses, and other responsibilities be damned).

I constantly wondered why my dad was obsessed with visiting. Indeed he had better things to do, and it was boring to be stuffed in a house without air conditioning or Internet. I had friends to IM, for Christ's sake.

Even after his divorce from my mother, Dad piled us all in his car and drove us to the neighborhood's edge, where abuela lived. Her home was only minutes away from our little pink house with the broken chain fence. It was a blessing for Dad and a curse for Mom. She knew it would end in trouble, and I hated that no one cared how she felt.

Of course, Mom disapproved. "That's the woman who your father always chose over me. The one who let his mistresses meet him there so that I wouldn't know. She doesn't respect me at all. I don't want you there." It was challenging to go against my mother's wishes. She should be number one in my father's life, right? How could a mother break apart someone's marriage if her role in raising her child was over?

Inevitably, the tias and older cousins labeled my mom as a maniac who was being ridiculous. Then again, when a Dominican matriarch stands before you, the best you can offer is loyalty. No one could do wrong to abuela, lest they have her seven children confront the said perpetrator.

I remember many arguments where I upset my dad by disobeying him and refusing to physically get out of the car once he was parked in front of abuela's flowers on the beaten-down lawn. But sometimes, I gave in, he was my father, after all, and I could never win the battle between right and wrong when it came to his relationship with my Ecuadorian mother. She, like abuela, also carried a magnetic aura that no one could escape—even if they tried.

Eventually, I turned eighteen. If I visited abuela against Mom's will, she could no longer run to the courthouse and give the judge an earful about why she thought it wasn't in the best interest of my siblings and me.

I'd watch my dad's face light up with laughter and merriment each time he added another tally to the notebook. Whether it was for his team or the opposing side, Dad and his siblings could keep the stress of their lives (i.e., overdue bills, marital woes, and their kids' rebellion) at arms' length once they were gathered around the Domino table. This sacred communion left everyone feeling at ease when they left abuela's house.

While some of her children visited daily, others came only when they needed money or wanted her to babysit a grandchild. She didn't mind and didn't reproach you for having "forgotten" her during the week. No, abuela knew her value, and she stood in it proudly, knowing that someone would come to see her every day, and it didn't matter who it was.

Dad was the one who came with a purpose. He would pull out his checkbook, line her bills across the old wooden table and adjust the glasses on his nose to begin calculating her finances. The burden of an elder child in Hispanic cultures is no joke, but my father never complained. Dad never told us to be grateful because others had less. To stop complaining because it could be worse. Instead, he led by example, and to this day, I still find comfort in talking to him about something that's seemingly going to end my world. When at the other end of the phone line, he says, "It will be okay," I believe him.

Everything was paid on time; she always had food, and though she didn't drive, someone was always available to bring her groceries or taxi her to and from appointments and church. Ah, *la Iglesia*. I suspected religion to be the glue between all the siblings in that house.

Though I loved her, I disagreed with her opinions on things she wanted us to accept as gold. Her beliefs were old-fashioned and judgmental. My opinion never mattered, though. Abuela was weary of everything that did not support her Jehovah's Witness theology. The Bible interpreted in a way that if you even wear the wrong clothes or think about a secular song, you'll be shunned. If male and female cousins wanted to spend a day at the beach, she called it a sin. That extremism didn't sit well with my cousins and me, who were already dissatisfied with answering to our parents and their hawk-eye view. "Leave us alone," we'd protest, "We aren't sinners; this is just how the world is now." You're too old to understand, and your beliefs are antiquated. That was what we thought but never said aloud.

Though I disagreed with her values, I grew to form my own type of bond with abuela. My eyes and hair resembled hers, and she loved me. Looking at her black and white photo, stately in every way, mounted in the hallways at all the apartments she had before buying the humble one-story on Sun Vista Way made me wonder: *What other secrets do you hold?*

Abuela was rarely angry and although she had survived a difficult life. Her womanhood began in exile from her folks when she refused to marry the man her father handpicked for her. This boldness to choose in her love life back in the 1920s spoke loudly of the type of woman she would be. It, therefore, came as a surprise to me how forceful she was with the grandchildren; she tried to impose on us whenever we wanted to make our own choices, and I didn't like that.

As a Dominican woman, do I do things the same way? No, and I'm not sure that I could. My beliefs are different; I want my kids to understand the value of their strength and individuality without fear that they're disappointing me. What I yearned for in my future was not the things my grandparents thought about in their youth.

Unfortunately, the reality of my upbringing only tangentially affected the traditions of my culture, but a lot did stick with me, including the language. White teachers raised me alongside middle-class friends in cushy, suburban houses. My sons are half-German and learning phrases in Spanish along the way, fascinated by bachata and increasingly more curious about what it means to be Hispanic.

Even with two little ones and another baby on the way, one thing is clear. I may not be a Dominican matriarch in the same sense my abuela ruled her household with a fierce grip over how people dressed, spoke, and behaved, but I'm still a Dominican mother.

I realize now that a mother's role is never complete. It's not easy to control a whole family, let alone an entire generation of people with their kids and problems. You can't tie a nice bow on that responsibility and shoo it away at their eighteenth birthday. Instead, you brace yourself for what's to come in the next stage of their life and how you can be there as their pillar of support.

After abuela's passing, the dynamic has only shifted mildly. People still gather at her home regularly and meet for tostones and their dose of weekly gossip. Abuela's adult kids, and now adult grandchildren, still have a penchant for the feeling they craved each time they entered her casita—the place she turned into a shelter for over twenty years. It speaks volumes to feel how alive abuela's spirit remains among us all.

And yet I still know nothing about how to obtain that otherworldly power abuela still has over her devoted family.

AN OBIT FOR MY GRANDMOTHER

Yahaira Castro

All abuelas are bad-asses. Mine was *the* baddest.

We called her Mamá, but everyone else called her doña Luz. She'd never even lived en la capital. No one from El Listin, CDN, or DR1 came to write her obituary when she passed away from stomach and pancreatic cancer. She was just a wife, mother, and grandmother to nine kids. She'd lived her entire life in Andres, Boca Chica, under the shadow of the town's sugar mill.

By the time I was born, her hair was grey with a broad, white mechón on the left side of her head. Her voice was a bit raspy, y cuando echaba dos o tres coños, it made everybody freeze.

Once, when I was eight or nine, I grabbed an avocado off a table. The fruit had fallen from one of the trees in mamá's backyard. I rolled it around in my hands and squeezed until green mush burst out of the top. Stupidly, I put it back, and not long afterward, mamá made a frustrated sound.

"Quien me cojio uno de los aguacates y le dio un apretón?" she yelled.

All the children gulped. Hands clammy, I stepped forward.

"Fui yo, mamá," I said.

"Fuiste tu?" she asked, surprised.

"Si, mamá."

My cousins scattered, abandoning me.

Mamá nodded slowly. "Me gusta que me dijiste la verdad. Los aguacates no se aprietan. Okay?"

Today, I'm an adult with a teenage child and still can't help but equate avocados with truth-telling.

Like many Dominicans born in the diaspora, I spent most of my summers in the DR and even went to junior high school there. My grandmother was my caregiver and teacher; la que imponía la ley. Disappointing her felt like you were crushing your own spirit. Take the time my cousin and I started a business selling Esquimalitos. There were multiple schools nearby, and we figured we could make a killing off the kids. We sold Kool-aid-type icies and did well, but we grew bored. We were teenagers and didn't want to be held down with the responsibilities of a business. Abuela saw what was happening, and before the clientele we'd built had moved on, she and my grandfather took over things. They did away with our product line and offered natural fruit varieties like pineapple and guanabana. The kids went crazy, and my grandparents sold at least a hundred a day. "Cuando comienzas algo, terminalo," mamá said. "Si no, entonces te conocen como irresponsable." Her disappointment was far more blistering than an angry hand.

When Trujillo opened up schools for adults who hadn't learned how to read and write, she was already an adult herself. Mamá went to one of them and eventually learned enough so that no one could take advantage of her. She started her empire when a friend asked her if she wanted to join in on a *sang*. At the same time, my grandfather had been in an accident at the mill and was healing in a hospital en La Capital. She asked her friend to give her the first number, which amounted to a little over three pesos. Mamá took the money and visited my grandfather in the city hospital. On her way back, she stopped at un mercado and bought as many viveres as she could carry. She made everything into frituras and put everything out on the tiny porch of the house the mill rented out to my grandfather.

A neighbor walking by paused. "Tu tienes una fritura?"

"Si," she said. "Comprame."

By the time I came into the world, my grandmother was doing well. I didn't know her as poor. The family home was one she'd built once she could afford to leave the mill's housing. The house was large, and the backyard was more extensive than most in that area. There was always at least one woman who helped with the cooking and cleaning. People who had business with my grandmother always went in and out of the house. She lent money at fair interest rates and owned a carnet down at the port. She'd been a landlord of multiple homes and ended up gifting each of her four children with a home of their own. Aside from selling yummy frozen fruit from her porch, she made cakes and donuts every afternoon to sell in a little vitrina painted light blue. They never lasted long. Maybe an hour, maybe two. She constructed a room on the side of the house where she sold second-hand clothes. The only time mamá sat still was at night when she watched her novelas, y si no había luz; she sat in a rocking chair on her porch gossiping with passersby.

Years passed. I went to college, met my future husband, floundered in book publishing and then writing jobs, ended up in California for graduate school, and boomeranged back to the East Coast in 2004. I was still lost when my mother called me sometime in February or March of 2005 because something was wrong. Mamá's doctor ordered tests to figure out what was eating away at her body. I was unsure of my place in the job market but clear on what I needed to do when my mom called. I put a ticket on a credit card and kissed my husband goodbye.

My memory is hazy about so many things surrounding that trip. I got to the house and found my grandmother frail. She hardly ate. Each meal could fit into the palm of a child's hand. Something was wrong. My mom had taken over the household, and I took over shuttling my grandmother to her appointments. She was happy to see me. I kept her company. We watched whatever telenovelas she was into then, and if I happened to step out to see other family members, she made it clear that she'd missed me. "Adonde estabas," she asked. "Te perdiste la novela de las siete."

I was the first one in the family to learn what was killing mamá. I remember sitting in the doctor's office as he examined the MRI scans I'd brought him. My hair was covered in a red and white pañuelo, and I was wearing a pink t-shirt. He didn't seem very impressed with me as he made small talk while studying the scans of a tumor that nearly swallowed my grandmother's stomach. When he discovered I'd gone to California for my masters, suddenly, the scans weren't as interesting. I don't know how I held back from roaring, *What the fuck does me going to Berkeley have to do with my grandmother dying*!

Surgery was scheduled, and more family flew in. I sat on one side of her, and my mom sat on the other. He counseled us not to tell her she had cancer. According to him, her spirits needed to be high. It was a pelota, he explained to her soon after. His tone was light. He even made her laugh.

Later, it took a hell of a lot of therapy before I forgave myself for participating in that lie.

We braced for a miracle that didn't come. After the surgery, the doctor was vague when he spoke with us. Luckily, she had a nephew who was a doctor and cornered him for information. We learned she'd lost too much blood on the operating table. She didn't have a lot of time.

When she woke up, she knew. She fucking *knew* what was wrong with her. She demanded to see the doctor. She unleashed a ferocious temper I don't think he'd ever seen in a patient when he came, and I am sure he's never seen since.

"Si usted me hubiera dicho lo que era, no hubiera gastado tanto cuarto!"

The day before she was released, maybe fifteen or so people made the trip from Andres to say goodbye. A cousin and I refused to leave before our turn. When everyone was finally gone, mamá was exhausted. She gave us directives on how to lead a good life. Unfortunately, she was so tired I barely understood her.

Except for one thing. I heard one thing loud and clear. "Ayuda," she said. "Ayuda a los demas."

That night, I asked my mom to give me something to help me sleep. I wanted to dive into a bottle, but taking a valium felt like the more respectful option. My mom and I collapsed on either side of her bed and fell asleep. Much later, a barking dog woke me up. It was a dark, black-out curtain kind of dark. The electricity was out. The fan was dead. The only sound was my mom breathing. A peace came over me. Years later, it's still incredibly hard to describe.

My grandmother was coming.

I haven't told this story to many people. I told my family and my husband. I imagined people wouldn't believe me because I'd taken a sleeping pill. I must've been dreaming! I was familiar with the Western world that didn't believe in the supernatural. I was schooled in it. And yet, that night, a wave of incredible peace and infinite love exploded in my being. Instinct led me to pray. Seconds flew by when I heard mamá's voice whispering near my mom's head. I couldn't listen to what she was saying. I only recognized the distinctive rasp. "Mamá," I said. "Yo sabía que usted venía. Yo sabía."

The whispering stopped. "Tu lo sabías, mami?"

"Si, mamá."

The mosquito net was up, but somehow I felt my grandmother's lips and only her lips against my forehead. And then, she was gone.

I don't remember falling asleep. I remember laying there and feeling incredibly grateful for that moment. The only way to describe it is it felt as if my grandmother had walked in with all of heaven, and I—an interloper—got a chance to be in that space for a brief moment. When I woke up, though, that amazing high was gone. I was anxious, believing my grandmother had passed. I told my mother what had happened and she said nothing. She didn't want to believe me because it was either too fantastical. Or, if it was true, then mamá was gone.

I called the hospital. The doctor was releasing her. My grandmother was still alive.

By the time we got there, I believed it had been a dream. But then a niece who stayed behind, greeted us with, "Mujeres, a noche la doña no dejaba de hablar."

My grandmother had gone to the house. She was upset about the broken toilet. We needed to fix that right away. And she'd seen my grandfather crying, and she was worried about him.

The toilet was definitely broken, but no one staying in the house remembered talking about it in the hospital. And to my knowledge, no one asked my grandfather if he'd been crying. He was a stoic, made to be a super tough man. If he were going to cry, it would've been alone at night.

We brought her home that morning, and before the next sunrise, she was gone.

It's taken me nearly twenty years to write any of this down. My memory of those days, especially that night, is no longer as sharp. And, I haven't come close to experiencing that feeling of pure and blissful peace. What's still true after all these years is I miss my grandmother as much as this corner of the universe would miss its sun.

Before, I'd been lost, but my grandmother's mandate gave me direction. After she died, I took on a job in higher education and managed to do the thing mamá told me to do: help people. I gave my brown students a haven in a primarily white-led institution—their words, not mine. I left that field just recently as I stepped into the Great Resignation. Whatever comes next, I will remember everything she taught me along the way, especially the last lesson.

Ayuda a los demas.

CONTRIBUTING WRITERS

Abril Peña

Born and raised in Queens, New York, Abril Peña is a writer, a social impact professional, and the eldest daughter of her Dominican immigrant parents. She enjoys writing about her personal experiences as a first-generation New Yorker, navigating her career and relationships, and trying to understand her multifaceted identity as an Afro-Latina. Abril works in nonprofit and corporate spaces advocating for youth, education, racial and gender equity, and financial literacy.

Amanda Ortiz

Amanda M. Ortiz is a NY-born and bred first-generation Dominican writer, polyglot, lettering artist, bibliophile, globetrotter, and human rights reformer. Her degrees in International Affairs and Latin American Studies unearthed a commitment to peacebuilding, transitional justice, and remembrance space/recovery initiatives in post-genocide societies, particularly Hispaniola.

Ana Maria Gonzalez Puente

Ana María González Puente nació en El Seibo, República Dominicana. Es Doctora en Derecho egresada de la Universidad Autónoma de Santo Domingo. Durante veinte años se desempeñó como funcionaria de la Organización de las Naciones Unidas en Nueva York donde reside.

Catherine Ventura

Catherine Ventura (she/hers) is a Dominican-American writer and educator from Paterson, NJ. Catherine holds a B.A. and an M.A. in English from Seton Hall University. Currently, she is a doctoral student in the joint Ph.D. Program in English and Education at the University of Michigan. Her research focuses on the decolonization of Latinx youth literacies and the functions of memory in Caribbean Latinidad.

Elinol López

Elinol is a writer and researcher from Washington Heights, NY. Elinol obtained her BA in Mathematics with a minor in Psychology from SUNY Geneseo in 2017, and she is currently doing environmental health research at Columbia University.

Gina Arias

Gina Arias is a Brooklyn-based, Queens-born, Long Island-raised writer who centers on Blackness, punto. As a youth, she spent her summers in DR. She has had a wonderful life thus far and has always been ni de aqui ni de alla.

Jhoselin Perez

Jhoselin Perez is an immigrant, daughter, wife, mother and writer. She was born in the Dominican Republic, but emigrated to New York at an early age. She loves to write poetry, memoirs, and novelas.

Koylan Massiell Gomez

Koylan Massiell Gomez is a poet and writer born in the Dominican Republic and raised in Corona, Queens. Koylan graduated from Hunter College with a major in Creative Writing. Her writing explores her Dominicanyol upbringing and represents her dual identity as a young Dominican immigrant. Today, Koylan is the proud mom of two beautiful school-aged children and resides in New York City.

Mary Gomez

Mary Gomez is a Dominican-American writer born in Puerto Plata, Dominican Republic. She graduated Magna Cum Laude with a bachelor's degree in communications from The City College of New York. She obtained her master's in school psychology from Long Island University and worked for the NYC schools as a bilingual school psychologist for 30 years.

Nivi Canela

Nivi Canela is a queer BIPOC writer, performer, and creativity coach from Union City, NJ. She is the creator of Happy Song Time musical improv and Naked Broadway Cabaret, a virtual musical theatre-themed cabaret centering LGBTQIA BIPOC performance art. She currently lives in New Orleans.

Susana Kuehne

Susana Kuehne is a program manager, writer, and mother. She earned her undergraduate mechanical engineering at the University of Rochester and her masters from Virginia Tech. You can find her work online at Scary Mommy, Her View from Home, the Women's Fiction Writers Association, the International Thriller Writers Big Thrill Magazine, etc.

Yahaira Castro

Yahaira Castro is an aspiring Dominican-American writer and producer. She was born in New Jersey and received her B.A. from Rutgers-New Brunswick in History and a Masters in Journalism from the University of California, Berkeley.

www.ingramcontent.com/pod-product-compliance
Lightning Source LLC
Chambersburg PA
CBHW071358200726
48294CB00004B/1209

* 9 7 8 1 7 3 7 2 4 6 7 7 0 *